YEAH NO

Jane Gregory

The Song Cave

ACKNOWLEDGMENTS

Versions of some of these poems appeared in *Company, Cordite, Critical Quarterly, The Denver Quarterly, Elderly, Erizo* (with a translation into Spanish by Ricardo Cázares), *Jubilat,* and *OAR.* Much gratitude to the editors of those publications.

Published by The Song Cave
www.the-song-cave.com
© 2018 Jane Gregory

Cover image: *Capri Battery* by Joseph Beuys © 2017 Artists Rights Society (ARS), New York / VG Bild-Kunst, Bonn.
Photo credit: Stiftung Museum Schloss Moyland / Maurice Dorren

Design and layout by Janet Evans-Scanlon

ISBN 978-0-9988290-2-9
Library of Congress Control Number: 2018930687

FIRST EDITION

[.]

\

TABLE OF CONTENTS

.:.

for Julie

YEAH NO

•

That it goes from all
shall be well to oh
well

Knock knock

Everything is a pattern
of yesses and no

•

Now is only not otherwise
& sobriety's death   for the moon
is a licked wound,
the glimmering innards
of a ripped whale &
obscures the world's terrific exit   [obscure's]

•

Obscured, the world's terrific

[*Exit*]

I want to thank what is clear
for the grimness, what the
future's retrojection bore a hole right through,
the .commune where/as it currently stands

•

And what—

The moon thus shed
its singleness
as if it were real and behold:
The world's terrific

•

•

Why do I need my ideas   [*validated for me*]
          the index of prophecy is light
So that I understand
          the world with all its signatures visible

Light, icicles, feces, profit

                              Of the world
Was made
Panic
And then its exit
Imiseration
Graced

•

•

I understand where all this is going
so nothing I anticipate happens
except to what it happens upon

Everything takes great effort
though I am more
and worse than a coupon

For what will you go to this?
For what shall you like it?

•

Like what, the melody of thought; for   [?]
what, night through its own vision, green
-ing against the fallen
dark like hell in spring; like
hell in spring, how things feel; how
things feel wet, or weird, but aren't, not   [nigh]
made that way, only sensed?

•

Like what   [/ well that]
we are [as] makes sense like each
to their users and what
else not to be   overcome

Though here must be a bad vortexx
said everyone of where they find themselves
since everything

Since every known thing
only occurs to me each thing occurs
not to overcome what is else but

Hey   Everything   [Hey   Everything takes]
takes great effort

•

What of it stop it

Or what of it stops

•

What if it stops?

Whelm the field—   [Over/]
Whelp it

Whelm the field   [over it]
Yr face ok'd
My shame & by it

Help it

\

•

ACTION IS CONTENT AND CONTENT WITHOUT ANY ACTION IS DESIRE

There is a flashing forth by which
I enter your heart and instruct you: get me

to the brouhaha, the cry of
the devil in the cloth of the clergy,

the hubbub, bubba, go, scum
up the wildredness

and then you will see some of the light lifht
in the grass the moss was in the clover of

what everything is but m[in]e, dug
under the little I cannot instrument

, man, I have imperceptible knowledge
a lot, guys, and work very little

all of the time so that your desire is strong
as it should be to call attention to the title's

own: to unhurt with, be smart about, and
redact, while healing what makes you make them, your faces.

In *After Static* the artist is perfect, *after* meaning it's all gone
and we're after it, on it,

> like a hunter
> for   whom
> the • world
> is   just   a
> circumstance
> of   birds,

baby. There is that wiggles a but between the doubled
impossibilities, the dimpossibility that neither/nor's indemnity
restores. A worm in the mouth of a bird in the mouth of

So, science, something that needs doing, right, law, imagine it
undone, and *WHAT ELSE*, a wrist for your sleeves like love
unruins itself. Because there are no more books I will not will
what'll not write this fineness in which infinity well definitely
goes on in deafness as the blaze of the incomplete completes
you,

yon	civil
civilian	dear
yonder	and
wonder	such
vessels	as
wander	where

I had suffered a feat of logic and a cabin was lodged in your
nostril, Drama, within which the subject could neither pay
back, defer, nor default on those woes, floater, mine a

drift.

Here is what I do not have: all of it. Do some

Where   I
am   wrong
is   in

trying to provide experience, not take it, specifically, away. In
particular forms experience can either be learned or conferred,
or so they make

[make/less]

                                                        believe,
me, whose rocking is a mode and form confessing its astral ambit
and doesn't help the day-moon not appear as bird-shit on
the windshield as though as a mistake it could matter and be
taken, later, back

                              'neath the nother surface
                              atop the slight erotics of
                              the visionary turn, turn it
                              unto me on these days
                              but: all I can do is stuff
                              with my minds

•

I charged this language
in the lands of my fat

so bring low the rock
the dust it hides

in fire say this
sigh let the world

be stump riddled
with holes holes fill

the holes with its seed[s]
grossen your own things

juggle my thighs
the moon thru the treeees

•

•

What was learned by the waves
of their unending under wind
which irritates the sand was either not long
for this world or to not long for it

[Mess with me and will the sentence be
the baby of the best of us what takes
from   all   the   rest   of   us]

•

It must be— time, that unlimiter of suffering
unlatching itself around an occasion, by which   [cry]
I am obsessed, into which I am hurled and cannot stand

•

Being beside the self, paranoia is
looking in the mirror at nothing like my real face

Come out of the tent and do not be dead

I give up all the strangers and the not yet
strangers, for whom I only aim, to continue

the banquet of your rage and all our wrong memories
together, strangers to each other, all and each one

nothing and a band of nothing and others
nothing beside us

No, I am the unlimiter, untimelier   [!]

•

I cannot be but bothered with molecules, the study of
solutions, but infirm, fear inturned and that I feel
what I cannot feel I am proof
of concept, an abstract mode trying
to be practice despairing   [*to prosper*]
                    I am writing and describing
myself writing and suddenly

                                        [beside/ [a horse
                                        in a field] /where
                                        everything is / a version of /
                                        everything else]

•

UNTITLED, ON TIME

Having the manner of a
beast looking backward: nostalgia—herald, regardant—
for the ministered administration
plus   anguish, if   power   was
a vacuum you used on the rug
with   your   hands   it   was   less
effable,   but   its   language
much   more

like these are the bounds
by   which   I   leap
and here is a box and here is the box
you're in, by   which   conjunction
you   pay   for
things with time
though there isn't
a whole lot left
and if you can see the whole   immediately   it's   a   problem
and, like all problems, is given   is as a given, the gift work is but
doesn't   do
which is the opposite of a window
that is what it does, does what it
wants to be (outside) and inside
every word is a safe-word, each
one   anymore

•

The day felt it was an event.

The last is only   [last[`]s; last est]
imaginary but there is speed
without your time

•

Their ill to believe everything issues   [is issues]
from flesh the bells dry bones the wind
breath fouled by the corners
                              of their mouth
                              where they keep
                              how   to   feel
                              about   yourself

                                                                                    [herself?]

·

Soon it would be less easy
for him to contain
what they aren't in what he said.

Survivre, the sun
soon allied to the wound,
the word to the gesture
the living conceal, the living
conceals the end it protects

•

[What I shall come to rest]

I shall come to rest
in the crotch of the tree

[Jesus thought Of God / as I the Internet]

because i know myself God   [Your face wld put his out]
cannot be a man you *guys*   [giys / zuys]
and what else   not
everything takes great effort right
and is in my nature
to be wrong and redeemy   [about the wrld]

•

[so] i've given up   [so wronged,]
all your gentleness / for you try hard

to take it back   for when the dead
equal all created and the archive

lives for itself and on what decays
the map of decay, and if still

all my feelings go about
and I just cannot, or tell how early it is

to try anymore to feel how it's so late
or what if only I am the way

I think things are, weird,
how things seem ways,

how some pleasures are not good
for you, work.

•

•

Something is going on

Let me tell you what I know
of my own mind

The basic I feel myself to be

•

No more but just noise for the
Maintenance of confidence

To focus the sun on underborn whiles
In but also on whichever language dead life runs

[*In   but   also   an*
Whichever   language
Dead   life   ruins]

•

                              After a deep silence I neither listened to nor left
When sense was a spoon in the brain   I was a prince and I want to go home
just like you know   isn't it just this that there is   or isn't there just
nothing else   cruelty built   a bird's nest out of birds or declaratives
lie the birds on the field   to keep memory elsewhere
I was in the woods and all I want   's in the woods to be in the
woods where everything is

ambiguous from inside this transition and the moon just goes behind that cloud
just like the point is the same as its ruin and why not ruin everything, everything
that waves and every single wave to indicate a first awareness of its own death
tenderer tenderer now
now grief's beach a great offering to which I am not bolted a drowning
having borrowed one self's becoming and another's un

insofar as love is about death
one has observed the efforts of the tide and then directly seen the eyes of the wolf
and then that whole wolf relinquish all the difficulty in how difficult it is to be
a wolf, as it is so difficult to be a wolf, betides. Because I am nothing it is im-
possible to hate me for saying, say,

The Book of Memory and Death was a lyric subject after the death thereof
in a prose lyric compared to a painting. And already I'm at the wrong party
and everybody is an audience that hates me. The painting is "Niagara Falls." Very
well, the party is the noise going on and on.

Tenderer, tenderer now.

Now I went to look after 'self' in the index of one book as a beginning. I described myself as thinking of inventing the self as a thing to be indexed. This just isn't going to do it.

I forgot to observe all of the first things you would never, mean –while just this baby was.

I want a thought to rally us, to think it. Think how everyone too is doing something at once, really really good, that begins to be an understanding for a lot of others. You are reading this if you don't understand. It is almost, urn, as though I never was.

Spend all your time willing and get heavier and heavier at the elbows. Bury your hands and just keep burying them. I think I am becoming a hero or this is what it feels like.

BOOK I WILL NOT WRITE IN WHICH TED SAYS

*IT IS REAL
AND ETERNAL* and tries to keep it that way
in the comment feed beneath the dream
of the ferocious dolphin where then there
became an invitation to a new phase which
I accepted by going through and just
beneath it was trending: world of THE
END in a figurative but diminutive
alphabet including triangles black widows
probably snake eyes that thus configured
said millennia are real and life is easier
if none of my desires are for me until
whatever thought had kept for itself went
into an extant room to found a new tense
a new way of willing the future's end and
then the drums came down from the sky
as though not everything were not
ok and out of the rend slippery and day-
lit one washed up on the shore of the
bay to vomit that

       'suasion dispatched by
       the gesture's only
       aspiration forgivin' an
       irony like I can avoid
       by haphazarding it
       as a wizard who wills
       that I woulded it

•

The real future is a joke / For my friends / You see that

the profit's phatic, the vate
vatic,   the   states,
s   t   a   t   i   c

And profacie was prior to speech, the mistake the assumption it function'd as though what happened'd happen'd first in speech, when speech only suffers from what happens. It[']s suffering forges it, we thought

•

Since the gossip of villians to the last
has gone to bed—

[—*spell*
-*bind*   *go*
to   *bed*—]

what change, a rustle, suffers the face,
the wind, a mouth or noise, linens on
the street, or word—From the gossip
of villians *the king's ear does come*—

What?

Yes, and little else

•

To grant them but understanding—
explain well the beast without
becoming it—such that claws   [call]
at the crawling towards speech,
a figure by whose flicker it
forges what nothing maintains

•

And suffers like speech from what happens. All claims
[are] false, irritable with fear, desire. We think—but once,   [ear; err]
we seek to know—and from there we go
to the matter, bother of—

                                        of reason.

                                        What's the matter?

                                        —to the bother   [*we ok?*]
of reason what's the matter

•

•

> [worms, unearth
> ly good, like
> wood, worms,
> ~~whose~~ who's gd
> would will to
> wilt and do what
> thou whilt for,
> [w]hell,
>   I'll, uh—]

every con
cept's a spell
to will its / own exception

•

•

This is a book of paranoia obviated by paranoia   It exists as a delusion scrapped
by reality   It is called RUIN HATH / THEY HAVE ME   It worries:

> what if they this
> this they may see
> and begs of them
> Will you time let
> my thoughts wan-

der   Be done with me o time fermented time   For Ruin hath ruined / Everything
/ Adds up / To nothing do you / Really not know / Harms & fears / What you are
doing?   The book's calmest form is, well, I'm but a medium for ideas and in truth
the ideas too are just medium, regular   This is a book of greetings because its source
experiences everything as a confrontation that must be recognized to first
face then evade: Hurt, a hi / to that / grief for which / the word / is reserved   It is
a book of Rain, falling / on tenterhooks / overer the gate, and the gash is to go
through it   I didn't write this book because I heard they were nearby and said "ok"
and tried to devalue this object a second time, to preempt and follow the first, the
one they executed   Paranoia reveals the gyres of time and that the
maximum brain's script is to minimize the body   The script is filled / at the pharmacy /
on the way / to go home / to / • /   A lean, for there is a lean to the world so lean
against it   Really it's nothing to worry about, which makes us think
nothing's real   Nothing, like everything, is measured in units of media, as I am
a unit whose measure is taken by the ideas they put me through   Oh why are they
only thinking all my thoughts for me   But we can / get anything / thus must
/ be home / to receive it   I was at home when they came and I shoved the draft
of that book in the mouth of the VCR   And could have retrieved it but didn't,

afraid what might have been shown when it played, for What if they this this they may see that they'd a failed escape before them, I am that   A failed escape from what you heard I live in, a unit   And as it, I live in it, as a failing state lives in a failing state that to live escapes   So they let me read you the end of the book, convinced, beside myself, I didn't write it: /•/ So I met / my mill / in the death / for planets / are corporations too

•

•

Because of the wires and because I am afraid
we use too many invisible forces
the invisible forces   get weepy

about my ignorance, circum-
agitate the reft, boss the ether nether
from whence I pass, stupidly a person

apace the upper worlds
whose late effect is realized
as the thrown knowledge that:

I forget but in the face
of it I do, person, so whatever
sincerely you have to show up for, substitute,

it must be with visible relinquishment at the speed
of swans—the wolf—hope, whathaveyou sent up
with other plusses and [do] still not become uncomfortable

•

to be around, get with, neither impose your
relinquishment on others, either your ambition, oops,
but since, I am it—confident— that I am not,

what it meant as another meanness,
and out, far out, *out of little, not much*
not whirlwindy nor special, alive   [special,coma,alive]

•

and I don't want to work
on what's prepared for never

to end and wonder can you
feel my love point *from many a wondrous*

grot and secret cell and having aftered it let us
go come yes to have to truly have empty space   [uninvaded sleep]

for her monument

•

PROFICES   [*Whthr or not I have a sense of it, young history, I hate it.*]

•

Driven to no tone

•

Water strung out on the stones,
wind wrung you are rising

As will for all that doesn't   [*As will / for all /['t] doesn't*
                                                 will / what is / πH]

leave, nor, figure, you [out]   [Leave.]

                              [*Like what you have you have figured*
                    out of and taken away from everywhere else, or what you
                    leave, (it) figures, forms you, builds you out. Yes, each idea
                    is the lapse of everything and [   ] what falls fell first
                                                  [*sometimes*]
                                                  [*then*]
                                                  [*pictures of*]
                    from the lips. A bell, depending from its branch. Although
                    hollow, there's a figure for what there was no image for. In
                    it's all that / what you have— ▮▮▮▮▮▮▮▮ *fig leaf,*
                    credit-lapse, time-/score, vice versa—as]

[as] all terminus w/ no drive

Or risen a figure solidly wasted

•

Neither put forth
as a specific soldier My face

surprised / by the hand that put
something in him

My mouth surprised by the hand that put

My face is chang't but my head's the same

•

This way it won't be for very long

Not for much
will the flayed be
sucked up thru a straw

What gets shoved in my mouth
when [you] speak
to the dead   [across it]

For much longer   [Not for much longer]

Whthr or not I have a sense of it, young history, I hate it.

•

•

I manage an image of clay   of clay   which was
what was wanted   the   obvious   grey   and
thick wisdom   Hey,   real chaos   that gathered
non-concept   a point that is not a point
The   *"nowhere-existent   something   or   the   some-*
where-existent   nothing   is   a   non-conceptual   con-
cept   of   freedom   from   opposition   . . . the   concept   of
grey   . . . the   grey   point of the unreturned world
encircled by its wurning terd, because of which I
am sorry

•

in that I want to belong to the ocean
because of what it looks like to see
Money comma the point
has no magnitude but is still
the inception of a line and the line
has no point which is the portion
I've horded, is swarming

•

the bower made by agitation—

•

everything exactly as incomprehensible as the world
's recollection of the suggestion to manifest—   [something / Matter est.]
something—

                [something] in relation to power that is its own
                preposition, and something about the lights
                of many houses, blockchains, about making actual
                -ly nothing out of actually something even if that
                something is INVISIBLE BUT FOR/CES
                ITS EFFECTS ON THINGS and drained of perfection
                also animates what remains to ask what time it is—*how*
                goes the enemy?—what time, yet time, for problems to
                turn off,

, to understand better
and arrive at the ocean, muddy, looking sorry
at what I have, have that effect on—
I have a MAYDAY in restricted—space, too

·

something has happened to my attention, come.
something has happened to my attention, .com e

> I want to go to the woods where
> you live and remember the pull you
> felt while dying I didn't neither snap nor
> come to that life with which I will't
> would experiment

afraid what information will reach me so easily

•

—easlily like the rose's neurosis but whose
retroaction are these flowers of?—

are they fear or is it time to hurl beneath
the busking sun an upsplashed real that flares to tell
you in confidence that thinking is knowing taking
no object, the other way around, though all
terms are search—and am I working
on, and what is there still attends
you and surrounds that fern's furlure
as an error that understands its ground
and has it to disclose

> [like when and even though I thought I could live in
> an actuary nevertheless I would go on to ULTIMATE
> A TRUTH like a future too uninteresting
> for   a   profit   to   disclose]

or open   Can we carry on / its [way
-ward] sun under the sign of which everything
/ mishappens

                    like history   [the rules of truth]

is a mystery because it rhymes
with its opposite not/and really

•

no offense will love what I defend

                                        even unknown

to me

                    I will care for you

•

                    There will be no
discerning on which side's the twilight   [twighlight]
like the one we are in and when I get there
can I help / LET IT BE INTRODUCED
by the fanfare in the distance it isn't

•

[*Lo, I've you*]

LO, there is a world
that proceeds through discovery rather than
invention to the al—

[alley alley ocean free, *allye all*
-ye outs in free—]

go rhythm

Really a MIRROR
WITH NOTHING IN FRONT OF IT RE-
FLECTS EVERYTHING

[/ALL]

,

Stupid.

•

Seriously, go. Let especially that return be continually self-critical, like of the tendency to conjure forth the lost and the broken and then think the origin of algebra or what   -ever will not only or not even restore them but provide the grounds on which they will survive or will have survived to be replaced by what survived them, for after the / twilight, whichever one, there is still no sunlight thrown

for here is no reunion no bone-setting so do not
spend your attention

•

FOR I WAS USING MY FLOOD VOICE THEN FIRE STROKE
TO DETERMINE WHAT FORCE IS BUT IS NOT EXPRESSIVE OF

when the order was *make pentagon*
and the reception of the order went—
through storm—*what do you think*
I am doing looking at my phone

•

HUSH, NUGGET, whilst drummed to the held
center, neither horse nor rider, a river under
water runs its course, whose manager's an image
thereafter, thereafter I manage only that

•

                                    so maybe
I'm going to the woods to make a coterie
and as a change IT WILL BE SO TOTAL that we
will have to call it a form / what precarity's perch
hurls when party, beast are hard to be so maybe

                                                               [I'm going to the woods
                                                               because I can break it
                                                               down]

•

or show me what doesn't depend (*weather's rush
deepened*): I have to go (*earthy bliss imbowr'd*): Call
me back

[…]

•

•

For the remainder give
us not your nothing
at the core of it, nor
your spiral unfurled re-
vealing horizontal space,
a blanket

•

But bid the wings you send to lift
the universe by its corners

Suffery then as a bellow from the blue sky
of having so little range

                              [yeah no]

                                        ~~*[patt asks shhhh]*~~
                                            [sic]

•

•

Silly, first you're clay then your face, Sissy, for it[']s net animates   [it's noose]
the neck, the cloth the marble it came upon. No, the door opens
to the edge /of the cliff and a figure climbs a tree felled by the sea.
                                                    The tree is a hole
in the world like a twisted fan, everything we see between. The seed
is in its stump, the *s* between reason and treason. They crawl
on the table through and up the brush and their fingers hold everything
like a trigger, [w]rung to ringing sound. And there is a little one who
carries a blanket to forbear the dawn, and waves.

•

•

everything is wrecked just fine but how do you know the raven to be no mirror to
the leaf

leafy shadow through which you know whatever you know

that nothing happens to

i know it was special for you, world, but I always have to go for I am the lung of the bio

sphere

and nondiscursive truth

yay, so toil, smart women be mean, my brain, refuse all work that makes more for others

my brain, obstinate failure of thought to escape itself, i am, bearable self, begun by the light

of the sky we are driven against, the sky, under which

each committee covers his feet in my house

each committee comes to cover his feet in my house

•

AN ESSAY IN WHICH I TOLD YOU

The bad infinity
is the one that goes
on. Like there is a past and I
remembered it like the day
of the death of Neil Young, the periscope
of Dash Snow

My life is the fossil of
me, or so conject'd the clam shell
of our acid trip, a tiny garden
in the garden and the world as it
was, was the worst war of all
crime

Still I could anticipate
the seeable you saw and even
thereafter, and once we had finished
cooking the substance it spilled
onto the paper in the shape
of a smiley face

Taken was
a picture and later some time
deleted it before the cloud
a purple spider predicted
then prevented my death

For it
was junk, belongs to the base
of our neck, gut, the juice the brain
receives, the port of—
the port, no return

The bad infinity
is the one that none
of us is having it.

Such was de-
dicated: it is for you for what
you're gonna do as you
think it and then,
it's for the dead for

ever

None of the thoughts
self affirm neither or
indict, when thoughts are
nodes of which it is put together then

The world
'   's the imp
of the possible and I
the only conductor in the pit

This is a poem
about the death
of John F. Kennedy
to which we bring the it
and the this it has come to:

There is a past what ended
when he died. Mine
when it died, and
when brother did
I had this other time
to be alive, or, but I could feel
anything

Before it
included me, for it
included me, I knew
suffering, the calm before
the sky's wished
an old bruise

Being dead, I play for you
what I'm scrolling through.

As it falls
out to think it
was different than it is,
then it is—how I see things

I see things
at two distances: your face
has to go through
the things it doubles over:
the curtains on fire
on the wall

                    paper

        The ground
can you smell what is
stepping on; the ground
heavy, can you carry
its weight?

        Like all burdens
are light, light's, or
words mean more
then you think they do   [than you]
for snow, money, everything's
medium's static's currency

The bad infinity is the one that goes on.

        None of the thoughts
self–affirm, neither end,
alright. Not matter can   [end alright; *end—/aight*]
never but ever what matters. None
of the indictments had happened,
even the ones that did

For heavy is the
bed, what buries
The bearer of the
future

Said here
are the keeps we played for,
you got, that got me that
I gave you to traffic in,
in drifts, in air's tendency
"to escape or be taken away"

It ended
five years after it died, when he died
he'd die in the grass, grass
the world used to have, sunset
from fire 'd take place, survive
on what didn't, anymore, there I
am gone
        to reckon with

On occasion,
the occasion, I have been
in the world but not. Not of it

How, lame,
the scandal of the sun
doesn't rise

How tiny—
mistyped joy and pain
as join—the differences and
little, they mean, or failth the occasion
what tried for fails   [faith]

•

Nothing is all [—and the matter—] that gets away   [away ok]
is all that what / the dead can't drive
and whatlike   the dead
with which

     I'm lousy / like what
     is known / or as the known
     and what the known is / told
     to say gets a- / way to stay   [ok]

riven, ruled, driven   [drooled]

•

To stay what is a way [drooled] against
nothing, or a way to say
nothing over and over, different ways

•

Nothing whose indifference matters to me
is built before the scheme and its transposition
in neon, [the schmeme], a no between
now and never—Shhhht.

           —Man I don't need

          a micrograph   to tell me
          it looks like   what it feels like,
          page,   break,   Drugs.

•

Though often I have felt a little weird

about the light and party to which it

would come, it is everything   [, *will come,*]

and sponsors its own ungetting

like autumn, autumn and its every miscreant,

(my friends),

[*Now that if we think of something they can de*
-finitely make it we can think of nothing at all,
but we can't think of it without thinking of what
isn't in it, and they can't unmake nothing et al]

My friends,

•

Help, fizzle my unbelief
until it bows, send a rainbow
around the lens, a tank in its halo   [*to govern*]

To govern-bent the coven
-ant but still, there
is something whose halo
is a collar for the world

Too remote to view
and the trouble
I'm having [,] processing, too

No visions, just what follows   [—what way and does wait—]

Them, My Friends, and even today

All they will carry   is weight

•

This book was written from prison or in hiding, depending on how things go after you accept this proposal and fund us and we do the thing and more than once at that. The thing was called *will our drone have feathers* but then my then-promising lover suggested *PLOP ART* and that's way better. We will begin with a small fleet of drones, simple quadcopters that have been slightly modified: an anonymous mechanical engineer will have installed a robotic bird's anus in each drone; the prop master, an amateur chemist, will have concocted something that resembles birdshit—wholly harmless, organic, and washable; and, unbeknownst to his employer (████████

████████) and despite his own ideological resistances, my ex-lover's brother-in-law will have been contracted to design the software that makes the drones operational and makes the drones' pilots' unlocatable. The first target was to be ████████

and the forces producing and securing him and the need for him on ████████

████ but our project wasn't funded in time. Here is how it didn't happen, and would happen again: the targets and the collateral reporters suddenly feel a drop on the shoulder or the head, reach to touch it and find a smear of, surely, birdshit and think thimselves unlucky, though some say it's actually good luck to be pooped on by a bird. Then, like popcorn becoming itself in the microwave or on the stove, the drops increase in frequency: the synthetic shit pours from the prosthetic assholes and

it   rains

down   upon

them, almost

like   wrath.

They are covered in it. By the time they collect themselves and stop their slippery giggling—for at first they curse and mutter, but upon realizing each is not alone, that they have been shit on *together,* some comradery and hilarity ensue, and we let them have it—to look up, the drones are flying—so high up that they *could* be birds—in formation away from them, in silence and with rapidity. The worst crime this book writes the story of is vandalism, for the worst that happens is somebody's suit needs to be dry-cleaned. However, it became so easy to imagine some terror, some actually weaponized fecality, that, well, you can imagine what the architects of these events were called. But the fleet would travel, was its own riot, from courthouse to port to police murder scene to some sexual predator's lawn, or office, etc. Although this describes an action aimed at politics, with a nod at biopolitics and another at the heavens we look up to when birds that fly through them shit on us, it is also installation art in the age of place's dispersal, they'll say. Sure, it's situational and performative, but it's a gallerist's dream too. Plus on quiet days the drones drop postcards and scraps of language: sort of like a horoscope, a few lines or a sentence will float into your lap surrounded by feathers the drone also drops as you eat your lunch on a bench (*what the fissure through which one sees disaster*), or maybe you receive a reproduction of a painting and we want you to make it meaningful to yourself. At the opening to which the art lovers arrive, well dressed, there is only a TV screen, an old one, not flat, playing static recorded earlier. Then the news comes on, for our target that evening is large. The news will be identical to the live feed we are and install, so don't you see and won't you, feed the birds so it's for the birds to starve the birds ꟼ

•

Surrendered by the cave belief became
its proof: there was no upperworld except
our exit from it, bright blue and radiant heart
eff you what's thinking and so smart

•

When I do this so you don't have to
look at me, or to this provisional language
run off the struggle to function toward which
I aspire and myself drag

•

Dragged together too what thoughts
are of: words, but not
just or always—

What's begun again to lead,
a satellite that sees itself and in the weeds

•

Words, but not just—

•

I said panic comes upon those who hate her
—Mean panic upon those who hate her

•

PROFICES   [*being disdained*]

>‹

Not to know but to go

on / Given up to throw off

this bidding and its bleak stuff

with which [the] [S]pace is

turbid, by which this

                space is chosen

that doesn't choose the thought

that rvns through it: what thoughts

are of they are   [not]

made of / what are thoughts

of, they are not made

≥<

Of what comes through great upset

to care for from where the threat comes

and corrupt comes the medium

confusion wept behind, left there

, so wiped and discovered whatever in the H

istory of Reason fans out before ya'

that you can get under like a tent

where great leaps are made,

leaked, like what [in me]

's made of   [sdeign]

being disdained.   [*being, disdain*]

≥<

NOW THAT I KNOW DEATH BY RESIDUAL TECHNOLOGY

Now that I know death by residual technology
Lust was the last of the first last things

shit on by the shadow of a bird in an airplane
ridden by the woman, [her] shadow woman.

Oh she does gather leeches, whoa,
did she say life is like light through a window

glazed by the frenzy of slime I came here to feel
, to be like I'm dying and that's the wor

ld whose backworld's zero-grade form
slathers its fleshy ills, on film, as a film

whose active form became an effect, its
forces actors   who station its train.

While watching the film in the tower
I saw from the bridge and seeing the bridge

beyond the screen from the tower,
I was astonished. The bridge

has increments. It is an eyelid
whose lashes scaffold the sky which, for $8,

the plane also googles through. On everything
we ride. Always it has been that everything

encountered is searched for later: "frenzy o' slime,"
"pre-fab tower." If it wasn't mine, it could be someday.

And because I think thinking is conjunctive, turbulence
is produced and stuck in your eye respectfully, thus,

next to my farty neighbor, I know how it occurred
to you when I was all like what is

necessary will arrange itself across this
wrinkled earth over which slithers the snake

that featured in the last, meaning latest, baseless
lie I told, the one about someone else's

recent fascination with snakes as a way of dealing
with sequenced losses of things that never were.

It was a lie I told to express love to someone
I didn't, a bid to undifferentiate it, a following

of the order to take social risks that came
running after the little ghost of a girl

in the hallway where also their refusal went

Well I ride these things so that thou may'st
know me, and I'll turn my face

who cares for that consequence of this decision,

made a puddle of your shame. I, a very big man
who makes a lot / of money—Try me.—step'd over it

all the same saying: excuse me I must do some memory
work: in the film artists are the dead returned

in an endless return after no return, return after no
return. Saying in seconds, you see. You don't have to

prove anything anymore. You are accepted. You will be
in your own new dimension. Hi. How are the impressions

I have made upon you. Well I like how you do
something good. Let me, I say, achieve the dishes

for you, the laundry, the garden, Cicero.
With your consent I answered the phone

from what didn't seem to be coming
any nearer until it did. It contained

some interference, the fault of its turbulent specters,
and the most beautiful letter written by a woman

imaginable. Remember when mom,

said she was lambasted by our dad, the bastard,

on a terrorizing loop, in the kitchen?
This is nothing like that, save for the real unrest.

Neither is it like my articular lerb
towards desire, whose hurl gives back

to the desire I have given you to give back to. Now
something should redden, there should be put

some flame to end the fire with, some blood
in The Hotel where I am fucking this

to travel with you, thus I have put here some companions
with which you will also travel. One, I am, is

the witch the internet is, boss of all our ether,
slid into our internethers, what relief

feels like forgotten, if violate
taken back, brusked to be unrisked, as I

had meant to call this PHILOSOPHY ON A [I can't com—]
PLANE and for there to be no apologies, but

of sudden assumption I've too much. The social shouldn't feel
like a frisk. I've a shamed and ruthless

something sold in case of all the mentionables. It is a matter
of confession, no more.

You see she works with what is the matter, works that
the leeches transvalue it in the isle or hall near

which you won't be long to arrive, will you, and stop
about the necessity of rejectable things,

regard them. Thus, saying—I has to a kind have—
I am against achievement. I would not

put a fountain in a pond for it knows not what
it is. It is I have, have to ungive up

That theory that goes from puncture to
future in which you have to need

something to make it and in what light.

To what belong the concepts I stop caring

because reason'd produced some excesses,
such as, some sense, so easily

it could have been otherwise, everything, and why
are they only thinking all of my thoughts for me, existing, and how

is it for them to know that I would not regard myself
in any way, were not other people, harmed.

•

This [_____] is an elsewhere to which I belong   [This [   ]
you, all—For I had let my shame make me   [*assembled ill/usion*]
dangerous, witness to your sickness who   [*de-loosed abandon*]
cannot   cure   what's   ignored   by   being   [*real confusion*]
informed. And   the   world,   well,   its   hum   [*renewed real/'s*]
mingbird is dead on the walkway, bent and   ["   *re-'lusion*]   ]
emerald let's go

                                                            [find/bury that there?]

•

[an ignorant army of avid ends]

•

What arrives,
boss, to total
vacancy, neon

Gods will come

[gods will comes]

you're welcome
vacant of origin

You're welcome

•

There is no inside
to the whild to the
body forged forgery
of my body
looking at its white young

•

As each self abolished in order to form
again from not what was thanked, or handed over—

> [—*order to form, form again from away, from again what,
> not what was thanked or handed over, form again not much
> but to coalite, coalite with where I can't come from*]

> [coalite, rare v., even with a z and a brand of coke; so
> corporation, coalacne [sic] and later 2,4,5,-T; and
> even *Europe seems coalising itself again*]

As each / abolished / in order / to form
and ahlite together where none comes from   *[alight together where nothing]*

•

Time existed to keep everything
from happening at once

and was running out, so
everything clamored to happen

at the cost of what was happening.

•

So as the redeemed clamor'd
for demand
So as the revealed revealed also
how to bear it

Paranoia was what
survived of what could
happen

in the moments knowledge passed through unapprehended, moments

gathered into
an *ignorant army of avid* ends

•

•

a man and the dog
i am

here i am
making a mystery

of a death / wanted
to be done on this rug

under you: danger,
oh & danger, dear

danger—fur lined camera,
what abyss's to be heard   [*v. what does abyss*]

•

Ta-da, a hold for what isn't—
potent on its rack—

all that I am
master of and let go.

•

TO HYPNOTIZE SPACE AND TIME

•

[1.]

Hide in   a lake house,   a   lake   house
with secrets   —habits,   as of politics—
fictions—   as of sciences—   yes
more that   (sci-fi lake-house) but

not as   "you look it up"
Science's   truth   can be   [—whose words / are images / of thoughts re-find]
measured   but unknown[?]   we can give you it, a

Uh simple   solution,   a   [a miscible *(sic/k)*]

Ride,   say I like it here where   it's twilith
and twilling but not twilight
and there's good tech that ancient
tonic I mean ancient tech is the future's

tonic, techtonic volcano / oh won't you
put me in you

•

No. P q r s t u v—

It is winter.

There is an s between reason and treason
And it isn't reason[']s

Why you are[!] / too sad for miracles   [Why are you?]
For, because / I just am   [Because I am / it is just]
An unhappy sundial, put   [, put like / a precipitate,]
By the universe as it passed
And belong/s to the *proffer'd seas*   have   [*your disease*]

You will see snows of the end / And then

You'll cry / But I'll have a little feeling
For you and so put
Your hat on my head

•

I came to as a middle between two emptinesses
        tantalos tantalos tantalos
        hellebore hellabore hellebore
and flashed forth the form perception would take,

[show the form his
perception would take (away)]

Though still sort of secretly, a ruby's shame
at its redness, or what the concept extincts
and I still have to deal with: recently, space,
time, and mind each a weaker force.

[mind / time and space]

But don't feel bad for me, reason
, which word also was an accident
that fell from the arms of men
that touched the bell and then the stone—

I said touch the bell and then the stone
As sufferer, I spread my talents for you.

[sⁿufferer]

Materials? the spirit is a line, like
Oh, what strings we have hung
the ceiling with, and spinners
to spool up each yawn, but down
pulls everything to it, and bricks
break the hest, the guest, to say so.   [*he . . . handlit hir and then's end'd*]
Keep trying, like the weird thing—it rests
atop your neck, there, to know   [what'll leave]
your mouths, what'll open—into which   [leave open]
goes light, what doesn't find the time, bent
-bound out the mind. Again it's weird,
like worth, a crisis, while fire will'd out.   [whild]
The dust's alive; when dies this accident
-al interval, life?, touches fire before what it's on—

•

Zero. It goes on up, a neck that
never stops. "bc what if a crisis and   [abuzz bc]
a consciousness and a cricis and a con
sciousness and of con
sequence of crisis, consishnousness?"—   [conshush/*nous*]

There is an audience
that is dangerous
to imagine, mostly,
and clearly, ex
ists

Do you still think
they are listening
and remember
myself

•

If laws were actually written
you wouldn't have to follow them
and the fiction of having them would
not exist until you wrote it; so what?
So what I mean as I write
the laws of the universe is that I think
you should do it, that already does
-n't anymore.

How much more clear
can I be—Shhhhhhh—
hear the wahter—
the internet / water used / to be

Fluid d fluid d fluid dt [. . .] Intern-
it is all over me as night's a solemn
background to a tree

[antlered to another, wired
to line the sky, our lake, O,
shadows, layer the paint 'n
stripe your thy?] [thigh? /
thight, thwilight, th'ight—
tight, thx g'night]

●

Though sense itself / cannot choose but/ suffragate to truth: [suff'r it, gate, get it]
Bye Bye / Bye bye love   *[Live from the land of the dead—]*
Bye bye consciousness—

What if God was Uni-
Verse—je je just a slab o'
thunder-dust—   *[Hide the path, dim the way.]*

Whisper, listen. Whisper,
Listen: no word   [here 's no word]
for truth but this
one word draws a window.   *[draws windows]*

My little scapegrace, just try
to roll your eyes while they're closed.
Awe shucks, said distraction to its presence in the room:
To the / Big girl / Go the / Spoils   [For which I only play @ truth]

●

At first [they] spoke only poetry (only much later did it occur to anyone to reason)
(Rousseau)

What's that, facts?
(Drake)

OTHER TITLES FROM THE SONG CAVE:

1. *A Dark Dreambox of Another Kind* by **Alfred Starr Hamilton**
2. *My Enemies* by **Jane Gregory**
3. *Rude Woods* by **Nate Klug**
4. *Georges Braque and Others* by **Trevor Winkfield**
5. *The Living Method* by **Sara Nicholson**
6. *Splash State* by **Todd Colby**
7. *Essay Stanzas* by **Thomas Meyer**
8. *Illustrated Games of Patience* by **Ben Estes**
9. *Dark Green* by **Emily Hunt**
10. *Honest James* by **Christian Schlegel**
11. *M* by **Hannah Brooks-Motl**
12. *What the Lyric Is* by **Sara Nicholson**
13. *The Hermit* by **Lucy Ives**
14. *The Orchid Stories* by **Kenward Elmslie**
15. *Do Not Be a Gentleman When You Say Goodnight* by **Mitch Sisskind**
16. *HAIRDO* by **Rachel B. Glaser**
17. *Motor Maids across the Continent* by **Ron Padgett**
18. *Songs for Schizoid Siblings* by **Lionel Ziprin**
19. *Professionals of Hope* by **Subcomandante Marcos**
20. *Fort Not* by **Emily Skillings**
21. *Riddles, Etc.* by **Geoffrey Hilsabeck**
22. *CHARAS: The Improbable Dome Builders,* by **Syeus Mottel** (Co-published with Pioneer Works)